Write
to Learn
Science

SECOND EDITION

Write
to Learn
Science

SECOND EDITION

By Bob Tierney with John Dorroh

NATIONAL SCIENCE TEACHERS ASSOCIATION

Arlington, Virginia

NATIONAL SCIENCE TEACHERS ASSOCIATION

Claire Reinburg, Director
Judy Cusick, Senior Editor
Andrew Cocke, Associate Editor
Betty Smith, Associate Editor

ART AND DESIGN, Linda Olliver, Director
PRINTING AND PRODUCTION, Catherine Lorrain-Hale, Director
  Nguyet Tran, Assistant Production Manager
  Jack Parker, Electronic Prepress Technician

NEW PRODUCTS AND SERVICES, SCILINKS, Tyson Brown, Director
  David Anderson, Database and Web Development Coordinator

NATIONAL SCIENCE TEACHERS ASSOCIATION
Gerald F. Wheeler, Executive Director
David Beacom, Publisher

Library of Congress Cataloging-in-Publication Data
Tierney, Bob.
  How to write to learn science / by Bob Tierney with John Dorroh.— 2nd ed.
    p. cm.
  ISBN 0-87355-246-6
1. Science—Study and teaching (Secondary) 2. English language—Composition and exercises—Study and teaching (Secondary) I. Dorroh, John. II. Title.
  Q181.T534 2004
  507'.1273—dc22

                    2004012355

Contents

You write it all, discovering it at the end of the line of words. The line of words is a fiber optic, flexible as wire; it illuminates the path just before its fragile tip. You probe with it, delicate as a worm.

—Annie Dillard
from *The Writing Life*

When asked why he became a scientist, the famous nuclear physicist Robert Oppenheimer replied, "Because my teachers allowed me the exhilaration of my own discovery." That statement haunted me. When I read it, I had been a science teacher for nearly two decades. My teaching style allowed little personal discovery on the part of the student; I was the sole owner of all the right answers. The exhilaration of discovery in my class had been washed away in a flood tide of commercially prepared worksheets and cookbook laboratory exercises.

Learning units typically began with an overview of fundamental principles followed by a focus on the details. I taught science as a body of knowledge, and tested my students on their knowledge of details. Those who were good at memorizing scored high, but only a few expressed any real understanding of the principles. I needed to find a way to focus on concept understanding and give my students the exhilaration of their own discovery.

The solution lay with expressive writing—the writing one uses to think through a problem. Anyone who has ever written a letter, a page in a diary, or an entry in a journal understands that the physical act of putting pen to paper uncovers ideas the writer was not aware of previously. Writing exercises both sides of the brain. More importantly, if the writer has ownership of the subject, the writer understands more deeply and retains what he or she has discovered for a longer

period of time. By replacing passive learning with active learning, through writing and cooperative learning techniques, I became a facilitator of learning instead of a spouter of information. My classes became student centered. The student-centered approach could be successfully used with students at all levels of ability. My enthusiasm for teaching was renewed. I no longer looked forward to retirement.

This book describes classroom-tested activities that effectively use expressive writing to further concept comprehension. Writing helps students think through problems. As they write they have a sense of what they already know and, more importantly, what they don't understand. This book also offers options for effectively managing writing evaluations without becoming swamped with paperwork.

Teaching and Writing:
Similar Endeavors

The writing process is much like the scientific process. The scientist first hypothesizes, then experiments, and finally revises his or her thinking. Most writers, as they work through a piece, initially put pen to paper without much concern for anything more than getting ideas down. Writers complete several drafts of a document as they attempt to get the material into a form appropriate for the intended audience. As Donald Murray, author of numerous books about writing, says, "The process is first a prevision, then a vision, and finally a revision."

Successful writers know their audience. They accept the audiences for what they are, not for what they should be. The primary reason many writers receive rejection slips is their failure to address the particular audience required by the periodical. By the same token, each class of students has its own personality. Skilled teachers take the time to know their students and present lessons designed for those audiences.

As a teacher, I was the toughest audience in the world for my students' papers. Many students saw me as the judge, jury, and executioner. Early on during my teaching career, the students and I would be obsessed with form rather than substance, product rather than process. Students would ask: "How long does this have to be?" "Does spelling count?" "What do you want me to say?" "How many points is it worth?" Many of them turned in third-rate reports that sounded as if they had been taken from the encyclopedia, textbook, or Internet. Student writing showed little evidence of creative thinking in the process, and their own voices never emerged from the text.

Successful writers "hook" their audience with an opening that makes the reader curious and anxious to see what follows. I needed to start every learning unit by getting students to ask questions and encouraging them to take the risk of getting involved. If I'm successful the students will assume some of the ownership of the subject matter. If they assume some of the ownership they must also assume some of the responsibility for learning. In my beginning years of teaching almost all of the responsibility was mine, not the students.

A successful writer shows, not tells. The effective writer does not write, "The landscape is beautiful." Instead, he or she describes the landscape, allowing the reader to decide if it is beautiful or not. By the same token, a good science

teacher engages students by using hands-on, open-ended experiments that require the students to make decisions.

The successful writer does not show off to the reader. He or she never uses vocabulary or information merely to indicate a command of such things. Instead, vocabulary serves to make a point clearly and to present information in a way that doesn't talk down to the reader. The successful teacher must apply the same principles to get information across to the students.

The successful writer is a master of the craft, a professional. The teacher must be nothing less.

The First Week
Building Trust

In my first years of teaching I was too anxious to hand out the textbooks and get going. I taught biology, the study of life, and I had only one school year to do it. I didn't know my students until after the first test when many of them received grades that discouraged future effort. I realized I needed to know my audience as individual students instead of as period one, two, three, four.

It took me several years to develop a new approach. By getting my students to write openly about their work in science, I was able to help many of them experience the joy of their own discovery. Even though I am now retired, I still regard this process as something very much a part of me, in the present tense. Here's how it works.

During the first week of class, I strive to create an atmosphere of mutual trust and respect. The students need to get to know me, and I them. It's helpful if they begin to see me as a colleague, even a mentor, instead of just another teacher telling them what to do.

A key challenge is to make students feel comfortable with science, which many view as

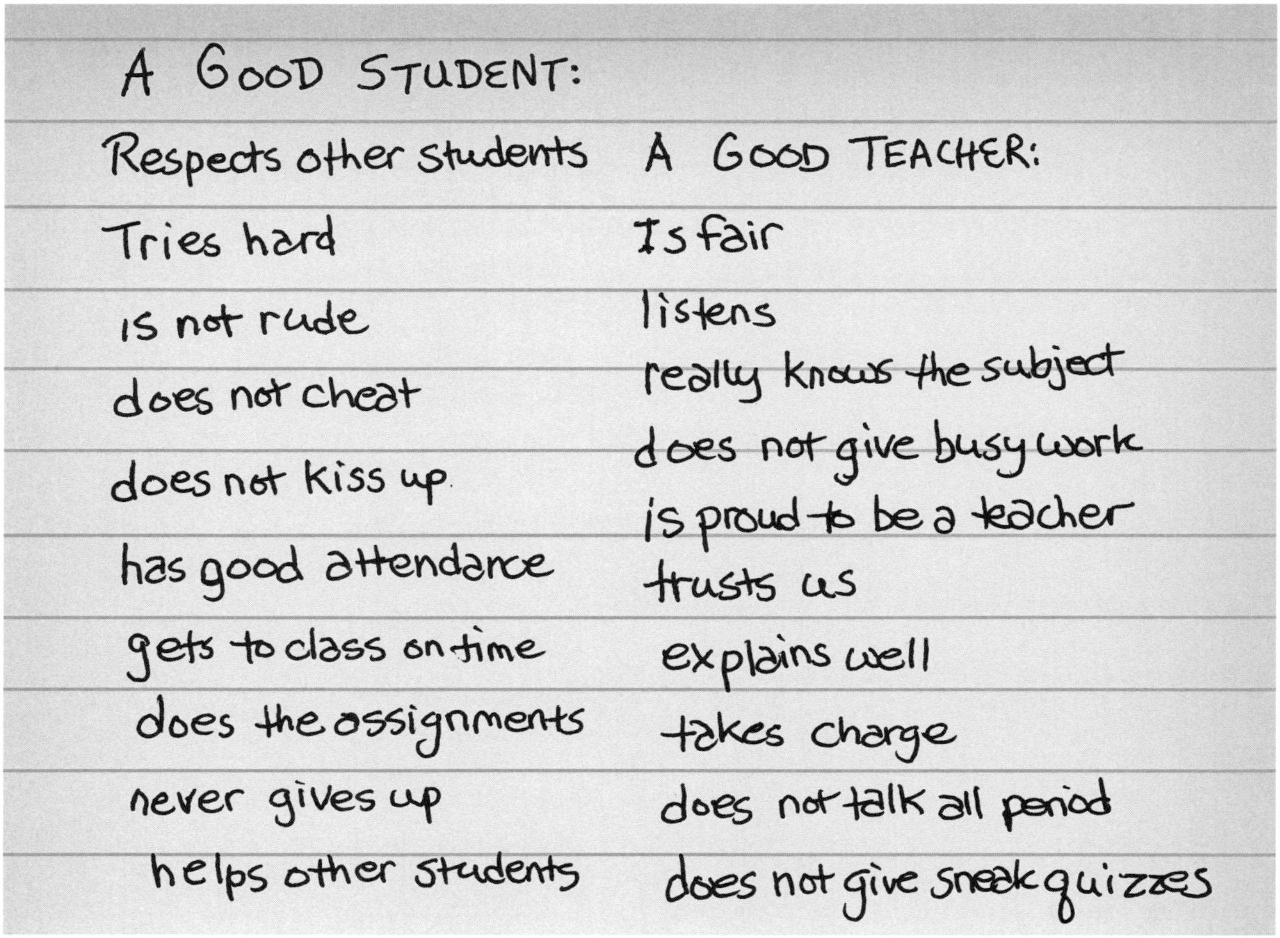

FIGURE 1. Lists of What Makes a Good Student and a Good Teacher

A GOOD STUDENT:

Respects other students	A GOOD TEACHER:
Tries hard	Is fair
is not rude	listens
does not cheat	really knows the subject
does not kiss up	does not give busy work
has good attendance	is proud to be a teacher
gets to class on time	trusts us
does the assignments	explains well
never gives up	takes charge
helps other students	does not talk all period
	does not give sneak quizzes

difficult to understand and unimportant to their daily lives. I use a variety of writing assignments to help them build confidence in their abilities and to convince them of the relevance of science.

Classroom Rules

Students are more apt to follow rules if they have some say in determining what the rules will be. At the start of each year, I divide the students into lab teams of three and have them make a list of characteristics of a good student. They don't get very excited about that, but when I ask them to also make a list of the characteristics of a good teacher they are eager to get involved (Figure 1).

I summarize the lists, and in order to build trust, leave in such ideas as "lets us eat in class," "gives easy tests," "doesn't give homework." The following day, the students select 10 characteristics from each list. Some teachers who have tried this idea suggest that using only five characteristics is better. My faith is rewarded when the students develop the final list, which does not include the items mentioned above. The characteristics of a good student and a good teacher are written on signs designed by students. The signs are hung on opposite walls of the classroom to serve as guides.

We agree to strive for the high standards we have set. I grade them; they grade me. Once each month, they anonymously give me a letter grade on a note card based on the criteria established on the teacher characteristic sign. They write a paragraph supporting their reasons for the grade. It's one of the best evaluations I get.

Getting to Know My Students

Day 1: What's in a Name?

After making a seating chart I ask my students to think about their names for two minutes. During this time they can doodle, cluster map the assignment, or close their eyes and think about it. This step is what the English teachers call a pre-write. It is an essential step if students are to write anything meaningful. I never give any writing assignments without a pre-write.

The students write anything they wish about their names for about six minutes. As they write I also write about my name. They then share what they have written by reading it aloud to the others at their lab tables. The exercise is relatively easy because students are writing about something they know and understand. It is amazing how much I learn about my students from this exercise. I am able to identify students who are apprehensive, have a low opinion of their abilities, and dislike school. These students would be likely to receive low scores on the first test, prompting them to give up on the class. That lack of initial success can cause them to become discipline problems as the semester moves on. By identifying these students early, however, I am able to ensure that most of them have a positive experience with the first test.

I read my essay to the class, allowing the students to learn something about me. This helps them see me as a person instead of a teacher or an authority figure.

Some alternatives to the "What's in a Name?" assignment are the following: "Give the world a grade today and explain why it should get that grade." "If you could be any animal in the world which animal would it be, and why?" "It is the year 2030. What are you doing?" The teacher also does the assignment and shares with the students.

One science teacher I know has the students write what they wish the teacher to know about them and what they wish to know about the teacher. The science teacher also writes, and shares, the assignment with the students.

Day 2: Learning to Be Observers

The students make a rough sketch map of the room and write a detailed description of something they observe in the room. They also express their feelings about what they see. The exercise provides insights into students' apprehensions and expectations as well as what they think of the classroom. For example, I found that a significant number of students, upon observing the preserved specimens in the glass cabinets, wrote passages such as, "Did you kill that little mouse and stuff him in that jar?" The specimens were a distraction. I placed them all in the back room and brought them out as they learned biology. It made more sense.

Day 3: Student Autobiographies

Students write short autobiographies of themselves as scientists. The teacher writes his or her own autobiography and reads it to the class. The teacher's piece serves as a rubric for the students' efforts. Sharing the autobiographies provides the teacher with an awareness of what type of science instruction the students have had previously, and more importantly, how the students felt about their experiences. The students discover that the teacher is qualified, but had a similar experience when first trying to learn science.

The following is a typical example of a student autobiography:

Science is boring. I am taking biology because it is part of the college prep program, but I hope to be a model or an actress some day so I don't see what this class will do for me. I never got real good grades in science because I don't like it. My sister always got good grades in science, though. In the fifth grade we learned about the solar system and that was sorta interesting.

Day 4: Why Are We Here?

On the first day of school, at least one student will saunter into class and ask, "Why do we have to take this stuff? I hate science." It's a valid question, which needs to be addressed. The question becomes a focused writing assignment that not only answers the question, but pays dividends later when students attempt to write conclusions to laboratory exercises. The exercise also provides an excellent pre-write for argumentative essays about topics such as genetic engineering or nuclear waste disposal.

Students pair up sharing one piece of paper. One student takes the position that science is the most important subject in the school. The other takes the opposite view. For the next 10 minutes they argue on paper. They do not talk. Using a kitchen timer to announce when to exchange the paper is a good way of making sure each students gets a fair chance. Figure 2 shows an example of what students might say.

When the students finish, they underline the opposing student's best line, or "Golden Line." They read the Golden Line back to the author and say why they chose that line. I ask for volunteers to share their lines. The Golden Lines are placed on the board and provide a basis for student-owned discussion. The discussion is triggered by a search for the truth. The search-for-the-truth activity teaches students to defend their

FIGURE 2. The Search-for-the-Truth Activity

Student A	Student B
You have to know some science in order to get a good job.	Pro football players have a neat job and they don't know any science.
Not everyone can play pro football so you better learn some science.	Football isn't my thing, but playing drums is. Rock stars don't need to learn science either.
They need to know the science of sound and stuff about electronics, don't they?	OK, knowing electronics might help, but this is biology. Why do I need to know about bugs and stuff?
Maybe if you learned about bugs you could become an exterminator.	Who wants to be an exterminator?
Well, you need to know something about science for everyday life, like cooking your dinner.	My mom cooks my dinner and she's no scientist!

statements and to learn to write in a more specific way. When, in my early years of teaching, I wrote, "Be more specific" on their papers, I eventually realized I was not being very specific. As an example, a student might write, "Everyone should know science in order to get a good job." This line, after class discussion, might be revised to read: "Many of the better-paying jobs require some knowledge of science; it's probably a good thing to know." After several such exercises the students learn to write specifically.

The search for the truth is followed by a homework assignment. The students select a point of view: science is good, or science is a waste of time. They write a defense of their position. Their grade is not based upon which side they take, but on how well they defend their position. The question, "Why do we have to take science?" seldom, if ever, comes up again.

By the end of the first week, I have learned a lot about my audience, but now I am more than a week behind the district curriculum guide. No matter, I have established a foundation of trust that allows me to accelerate student learning as the semester progresses.

If the students are to have the exhilaration of discovery they must become explorers. The first requirement of an explorer is curiosity followed by the courage, or lack of common sense, to take a risk. William Zinsser (1988), in the preface of his book *Writing to Learn,* says, "I saw that writing across the curriculum wasn't just a method of getting students to write who are afraid of writing. It was also a method of getting students to learn who are afraid of learning" (p. ix).

Varying the Audience

Each learning unit should start by piquing student curiosity. For example: I may place a petri dish containing a small polychaete worm, scraped from a pier piling, in some saltwater on each lab table. The students ask, "What is this?" "What does it eat?" "Will it bite?" I do not answer their questions. Instead I remind them we have microscopes and urge them to make a personal list of what they observe. Their observations generate more questions, such as, "How does it eat?" "Why does it eat what it does?" "Does anything eat these worms?" During my first years of teaching, the students simply wanted me, or the textbook, to supply them with an answer they could memorize. This exercise gets them involved in the essence of science, that is, inquiry. They are hooked, ready, even eager, to learn more. The students get all of the credit if they make the list, and none of the credit if they don't.

A chemistry unit might begin by asking the students to observe the wall chart of the periodic table and make a list of what they observe. The students ask, "Do we have to learn all that?" "Who thought up this idea?" "What do the numbers at the bottom of each square mean?" They share what they observe, and are allowed to take items from other students' lists if they wish. The students then write a paragraph about what the periodic table says to them at the time and place it in their portfolio or notebook. Making the list prepares the student to write. Then they write, free of concern about grade because what they write are their own perceptions. The writing generates questions. Students are ready to learn more.

Note that the two exercises described above require the students to write to themselves, the easiest audience to address. After a few assignments addressed to themselves, the students gain the courage to try their ideas on a different audience. Too often, in many classes, the only audience the student writes for is the teacher, the most difficult audience to address.

Sometimes, usually on a Friday, I ask my students to think about what they had learned during the week and to write a summary of what they understood. The audience for the summary is the students across the hall who are also learning biology. Those students, at the same time, are writing a summary for my students to read. All students are expressing themselves in their own voices, are focused on understanding, and are free of concerns about a grade.

Writing to a person in a picture is another way to vary the audience. The first time I tried this, I placed a picture of Miss Piggy on the wall and told the students to explain photosynthesis to her. They didn't like this at first, preferring to write to me because I already understood the process and they could use phraseology out of the textbook or encyclopedia—even if they didn't understand the terms themselves. To explain photosynthesis to Miss Piggy, they had to also explain any scientific terms they used. Thus, they had to learn the subject well in order to be able to teach someone else. After some initial hesitation, students began bringing in pictures of rock groups, sports heroes, and animals that they could write to.

Toward the end of a unit the audience shifts to me, the examiner. By this time the students are ready to be examined, maybe even eager. They have sorted through the information in their own minds, have shared their thoughts with others, and are ready to show off their knowledge. Their papers are more polished than those I might have received at the beginning of the unit, making them easier to read and evaluate.

Elements of a Learning Unit

What follows is an example of how the process approach to learning might take place in the unit about the cell, a learning unit used early in a biology course. The activities can be applied to any unit.

Starting the Unit

I place a large, commercially designed chart of the cell on the wall. Students observe the chart, making a list of what they see. They share their lists and are free to use items on any other student's list. They write a "before" paragraph about what the chart says to them (Figure 3). They understand the chart will say different things to different people. The students place their writing into their notebooks or portfolios.

At the end of the unit, the chart is displayed once again as the students retrieve their original paragraphs. They make another list of what they see. They write an "after" paragraph (Figure 4), but this time the audience is a biologist whose picture is on the wall. They must view the material from a different perspective. After sharing the new paragraph, they write another one with me as audience. In that paragraph, they share with me what they have learned. They discover that we have not all learned the same things, but we have all learned something.

Searching for the Truth

Each student writes one sentence they believe to be true about cells. We define the truth as something we cannot argue with. When I ask for volunteers to share their sentence with the rest of the class, I can expect at least eight students to share their sentences. The sentences are placed on the board. We decide if the statements are true according to our definition. If the statement is questionable the class is asked to revise the sentence in such a way that it is true. This can result in a student-owned debate with the teacher acting as facilitator. For example, a statement on the board might read, "Every living thing is composed of cells." Some students will challenge the truth of the statement by asking questions such as, "Have biologists observed every living thing?" "How do we define *living*?" "What is a cell?" After a class discussion the statement might be rewritten to read, "All of the living things observed by scientists so far have been found to be composed of cells."

The search-for-the-truth exercise results in the students becoming more precise in both their writing and their thinking. Several years ago, on back-to-school night, I overheard one of my students say, as she escorted her mother into the classroom, "This is the class where we search for the truth instead of the grade."

Hypothesis forming is a variation of the search for the truth. The students, working in lab groups, formulate assumptions such as, "All cells have a nucleus." They defend their assumptions to the rest of the class by sharing whatever evidence they might have. The other lab teams decide whether they have made a good case. After the evidence has been searched, they may have to revise their hypothesis by saying, "All cells observed in this class appear to have a nucleus, but there may be other cells that don't have a nucleus."

Questioning to Start a Unit

Many students are reluctant to respond orally to questions. Some fear their questions will be viewed as dumb, some are afraid to speak in public, and others are not sure of their answers. One way to overcome student reluctance is to have the students write their questions on note cards and place the cards in a basket or other

FIGURE 3. "Before" Paragraph

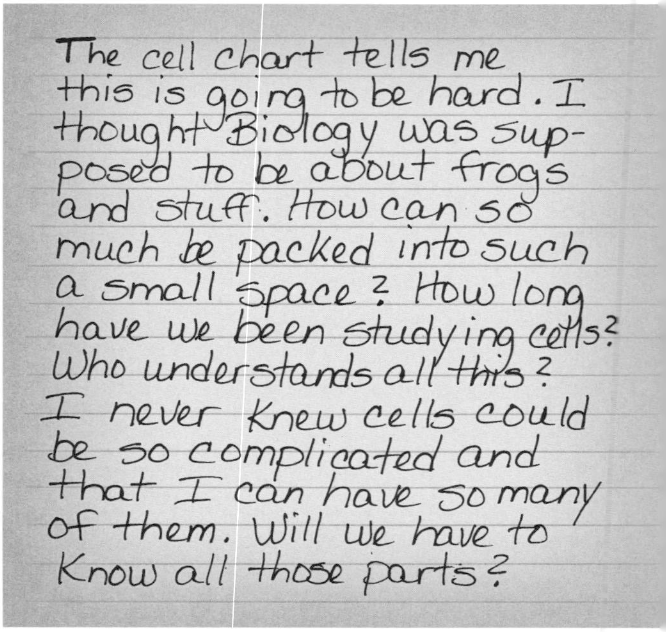

> The cell chart tells me this is going to be hard. I thought Biology was supposed to be about frogs and stuff. How can so much be packed into such a small space? How long have we been studying cells? Who understands all this? I never knew cells could be so complicated and that I can have so many of them. Will we have to know all those parts?

FIGURE 4. "After" Paragraph

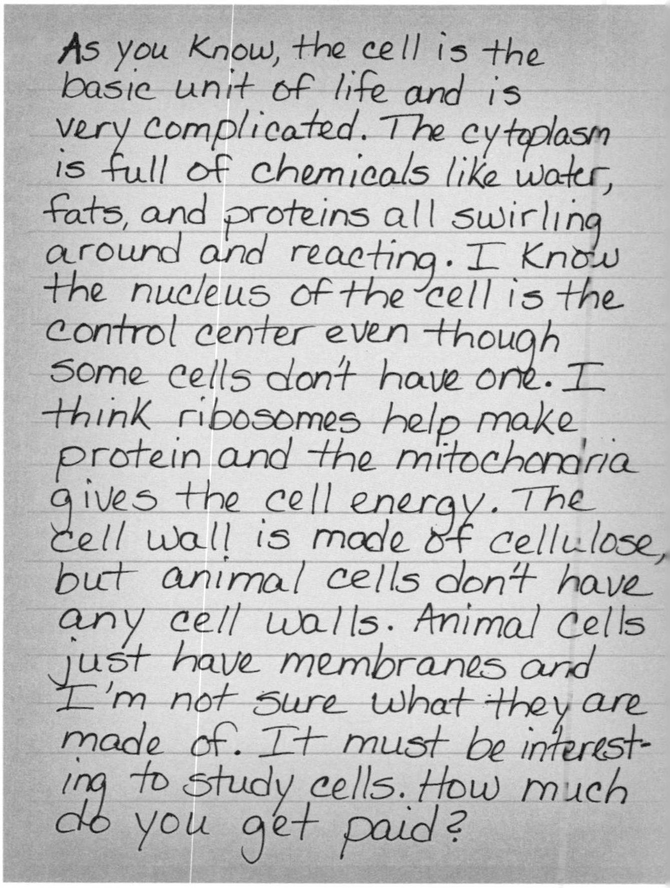

> As you know, the cell is the basic unit of life and is very complicated. The cytoplasm is full of chemicals like water, fats, and proteins all swirling around and reacting. I know the nucleus of the cell is the control center even though some cells don't have one. I think ribosomes help make protein and the mitochondria gives the cell energy. The cell wall is made of cellulose, but animal cells don't have any cell walls. Animal cells just have membranes and I'm not sure what they are made of. It must be interesting to study cells. How much do you get paid?

container. I purchased a green top hat from a costume store, called it "the question hat," and placed it on my desk.

The questions must pertain to the subject matter. A typical question might be, "How do cells stick together?" If I treat the questions with the respect they are due, my students begin to act like scientists, curious and eager to explore possible answers. They come to understand the essence of science is more about questioning than answering.

Sometimes I ask each lab team to pull a question from the hat. I give them about three minutes to find their *best answer*. They read their best answer to the rest of the class and we have another search for the truth—a lively, student-owned class discussion. My lectures, to a large degree, are based upon their questions. Those questions in the back of the chapter can be used in much the same way by placing the numbers of the questions in the hat and allowing each team to draw a number and decide on their best response. The lively discussion of subject matter is more effective than having each student answer each question as homework. It decreases my paperwork load too.

Lecturing

When I was in college, my education professors often preached to us in lectures with the overall theme, "Do not lecture to your students." When I first started teaching I ignored what my professors said and lectured as they did. I liked lecturing to my high school students. I had a captive audience for my self-perceived intellectual brilliance and my less-than-brilliant jokes. I was in control.

Unfortunately, I wasn't very effective. It took me years to realize I was not getting through to a large segment of my audience. Lecturing is a passive activity that provides the illusion of covering material while leaving out many of the

students who have different learning styles. The duration of the lecture often exceeds the attention span of the students.

Fortunately, writing exercises can be used to spice up lectures in a way that keeps the students' interest and also provides valuable feedback for the teacher.

Note Taking and Note Making

I adapted my own version of the note-taking/note-making technique, used by many English teachers, to my science class. It is similar to the Cornell method of note taking, sometimes called the "double-entry log" (Figure 5). At the beginning of a lecture, the students divide a page of their notebooks in half, writing "Note Taking" on one side and "Note Making" on the other. Using a kitchen timer set for eight minutes, roughly the attention span of the students, I proceed to lecture while the students take notes on the note-taking side. It is a teacher-dominated time. The students' responsibility is to listen intently, or fake it. When the timer bell rings, they stop taking notes and write their response to what I said on the note-making side. The only rules we have are that what you write must be clean (we define *clean* as something your grandmother can read), and it must be true. They read aloud their "note making" to the other students at their lab table. If it is desirable to lecture more than eight minutes, I then will lecture for another eight minutes with the students responding and sharing.

Homework following the lectures usually consists of a drawing that represents what the lecture said to the student and a "so-what" paragraph in which the student explains how the topic affects him or her personally. As I take roll the next day, the students show each other their drawings and read aloud their "so-what" paragraphs.

FIGURE 5. Note Taking/Note Making

Protozoa

Note Taking	Note Making
"Unicellular" supposedly one cell, but there may be a question.	How big can they get?
They are divided into classes by how they move. 1. cilia — hair-like structures attached to protein rods 2. flagella — whip-like structures 3. pseudopods — means false foot, it just flows 4. flotation — they go with the flow like amoeba or white blood cells	Flagella look the fastest. This is fun.
Protozoa 1. Take in O_2 by diffusion 2. Respiration by Kreb's cycle 3. Aerobic 4. Take in food by oral groove or just engulfing it	We learned that diffusion and respiration stuff in chapter 4. It's starting to make sense.
Reproduction asexual — splitting, mitosis sexual — exchange DNA, more variety	When paramecia just split in half, is that the cloning? Is cloning asexual?

The students realize they are all hearing the same thing, but interpreting it differently based on their own experiences and prejudices. This came as a surprise to me when I first began using this technique. I understood why so many students scored low on quizzes. They listened, but for many of them the lecture style is not the best approach to learning. By comparing observations, the students learn a lot from each other because the comments reflect different perspectives. I can determine what most of them really understand and whether I need to slow down or emphasize certain topics better.

Quick Reviews

Exit Cards

Sometimes I ask my students to summarize, in one clear sentence, the main thrust of the lecture. Writing a short, but accurate, description of a complex subject is a difficult task; even veteran journalists rate this as one of the most difficult aspects of their profession. In order to do this well, they must fully grasp the subject, weed out what is extraneous, and explain the important elements in a clear manner. As a result, the exit card is an excellent method to sharpen student thinking and writing skills.

I collect the note cards as the students file out the door. I place check marks on each card indicating I read it, and I might write comments on the back of some of the cards as appropriate. I place asterisks on five cards, sometimes at random and other times based on their content. The students who own the cards with an asterisk are asked to reproduce their sentence on the blackboard as soon as they arrive in class. The first few minutes of the class are spent in discussing the sentences and answering questions such as, "Is this what the lesson was about?" "Are the details in the proper order?" "Are they an accurate reflection of emphasis?"

Fast-Write Paragraphs

During the last five minutes of class, I sometimes ask students to anonymously write a paragraph describing what they learned from the lesson. These paragraphs provide valuable insights into what they understood and how they felt about the lesson. I can often use these paragraphs to adjust my teaching for the next class session.

Simile Reviews

Albert Einstein thought imagination was the most important criteria for being a scientist. Elementary teachers allow students to use their imagination a great deal while many high school teachers, believing they don't have time for games, ignore this effective way of triggering student thinking.

The simile review is one of my favorite ways to rouse students' imaginations and, in the process, find out what they understand. Similes, as we learned in English class, vividly compare things and point out what is similar about them, generally using the word *like* or *as* (e.g., "The snow was like a blanket on the ground." "His temper was as explosive as a volcano."). During the cell unit, I ask each student to write a paragraph completing the following simile/sentence: Mitochondria are like _____ because _____ .

A student might choose to follow the word *like* with, say, *Wheaties*. Describing why mitochondria are like Wheaties gets the student thinking about the subject in new ways. The student's complete response might be as follows:

The mitochondria are like Wheaties because they give the cell energy like Wheaties are supposed to do for your body. Both Wheaties and mitochondria contain fats and proteins, which are good for making energy. So, if you eat your Wheaties you will become a champion, but if your mitochondria don't work—forget it.

A variation of the simile exercise is to have students take large sheets of paper and fold them into four numbered quadrants. In the first quadrant they describe a plant cell they are observing under a microscope. The description is shared with their lab partners. In the second quadrant, they complete the following sentence:

A plant cell is like a _____ because _____.

Students volunteer to share and explain why they chose the simile they did. The class votes for the most "far-out" simile to describe a plant cell. Some of the similes suggested might be a walled city, warehouses, sugar cubes, bricks, or TV screens. Assuming the class chose TV screens as the most far-out simile, all of the students write in quadrant three what it would be like to be a TV screen, or to be in a TV screen. They share what they have written.

For quadrant four, the students are directed to write as fast as they can anything that comes to their mind when I give them a word or words. The words in this case would be *plant cell*. Quadrant four is also shared. The following is an example of what might be expected:

Quadrant One: *The plant cell is rectangular with a lot of little green dots around the edges. It has a clear, wall-like structure around it to keep everything inside. I can't see a membrane, but I guess it has one. I don't see any nucleus. Aren't plant cells suppose to have a nucleus?*

Quadrant Two: *A plant cell is like a walled city because it has a thick protective covering that keeps all the bad stuff out and the good stuff in. Real walled cities have a gate someplace, but the plant cell gates must be too small to see. Plant cells don't have guard towers though. I wouldn't want to live in a walled city that was built like a plant cell.*

Quadrant Three: *If I was in a TV screen I would get very hot and I would have to dodge all*

those tiny electronic dots that bombard the surface, but maybe that only happens when there's snow, ha, ha. I guess I would sleep when the TV is turned off, but getting woken up by a jolt of electricity wouldn't be any fun. It wouldn't be any fun having people watch you all the time either. Changing the stations all the time would drive me crazy.

Quadrant Four: *The plant cell, like most cells, has a nucleus, cytoplasm, and all that other gunk. But the plant cell can make its own food. That's what all the little green things, the chloroplasts, do. TVs get their stations changed a lot. Plant cells are always changing inside too, like when they make sugar and reproduce and all that other chemical stuff. TVs get their energy from electricity. Plant cells get their energy from the sun.*

Notice how the writing has changed between quadrant one and four. In quadrant four the student has stretched his imagination a bit and has included material from his lab partners. Most importantly, the student has done some thinking.

The Reading-Writing Connection

The information explosion has made the prospect of "covering" all the material in a textbook during the school year increasingly unlikely. Education researcher Mary Budd Rowe found that the average high school science text introduces seven to ten new concepts per page and between 2,400 and 3,000 symbols overall ("Rethinking Thinking in the Classroom," *The Science Teacher,* Dec. 1988, pp. 22–25). She calculates that teachers who wish to cover an entire textbook must introduce a new concept every two minutes. Too much emphasis on the text results in teaching science as a body of knowledge.

Text Reading

Reading, like writing, is a process. The wise teacher approaches the task of text reading in a manner that will both enhance student understanding of various concepts and improve reading skills. New material is best learned in small, positive steps. It is better to assign a five-page segment of reading than to assign the entire chapter. The students, with the teacher as facilitator, should review what they already know about the material prior to reading the material. As they read the text they should "interact" with it in various ways. They might write paragraphs contrasting, comparing, or associating what they read with what they know. They might compile questions that go beyond what they have read. Students who interact with the reading material will comprehend more fully what they read.

In our unit about cells, I might approach a reading assignment as follows: Before reading the students survey the main headings, scan the charts, and write a paragraph explaining what they believe they already know. These paragraphs are shared with others at their lab tables. Each lab team compiles a list of questions they hope to have answered as they read.

I often place a list of 10 vocabulary words from the reading on the board. The students write, without looking at their book, what they think each word means. They respond to each word. If they do not know what the word means, they may write, "I have no idea what this word means." The students share their definitions with each other; I do not define the words for them. After reading the material, the students redefine the terms and share them once more. If the words are necessary for understanding a concept, I might give them a nonthreatening vocabulary quiz for several days in a row.

Reading Logs

As students read their textbooks, they have a written dialogue with the author. On a sheet of paper, they raise questions, argue, find Golden Lines (as described on p. 7), agree, compare, and contrast. An example of a reading log might be as follows:

I've heard of photosynthesis before. I figured it must have something to do with plants and I was right. How can a cell get energy from glucose? I never knew chlorophyll was so important. The author doesn't tell us how it makes sugar. What else does it do? All this chemistry stuff is confusing and I don't think I can memorize all these new terms. Will they all be on the test?

When the students arrive in class the following day, they read their logs aloud and discuss their observations while I take roll. Students who did not do the assignment apologize to each other, not to me. This is more effective than threatening a sneak quiz, which implies a lack of trust on the part of the teacher. Writing to learn is only effective in an atmosphere of trust.

The logs are interesting reading—students often express their confusion, and we can structure the class to address these problems. In my early years of teaching, students would never admit to not knowing something for fear of receiving a low grade. When they admit their lack of knowledge now, it says three things to me: (1) They trust me, (2) they must have searched their minds for what they do understand, and (3) they are ready to learn.

A teacher can use writing exercises discussed in previous sections to follow up on reading assignments. Students might write a one-page summary of the important ideas, a "so-what" paragraph, or a simile exercise.

Lab Report Writing

Some science teachers have difficulty using hands-on activities that ask students to find an unknown, design a procedure, or formulate a hypothesis. The typical class period seldom allows time for elaborate lab exercises. Science teachers, with many classes and several preparations, often find themselves at school long after everyone else has gone home. Evaluating lab exercises adds to the paperwork load. Commercially produced laboratory exercises rarely allow students to formulate the question or the hypothesis. Cookbook procedures, fill-in-the-space results, and conclusions ignoring the "why" erase any exhilaration of discovery. Students, with no time to reflect, focus on getting the task completed, regardless. The grade becomes more important than understanding the exercise.

After some trial and error, I came to understand that report writing was a process learned over time. It was unreasonable to expect that students would be able to write a readable report on their first attempt. I altered my approach to focus on the components of the report instead of the entire lab. The students wrote the entire lab report each time, but I focused on, and graded, only the component being stressed at the time. After several weeks I was able to ask the students to write up formal lab reports and expect first-rate results.

Organization of the Lab Report

Simple exercises, designed to emphasize organization, can be used as a first step. For example: Each lab team might find four different leaves on their table when they arrive in class. I pose the question, "Which of the leaves on your table will go the farthest in a windstorm?" The lab teams formulate a hypothesis, outline a simple procedure, record their results, and write a conclusion. The focus is on organization only. If the students have all of the components of a lab report they get a good grade. It might take two or three of these simple labs before the entire class understands how a lab report should be organized.

Writing Lab Questions

The first, and often most difficult, task in any experiment is to ask the right question. Reversing the lab organization can provide practice for refining questions. Sometimes I provide students with only the conclusion of a lab report and ask them to determine what they believe the original question might have been. Other times I might do a demonstration activity in front of the class. They write questions and share them. I place their questions on the board for discussion. The students decide which question is most appropriate for the procedure they observed.

In our unit about the cell, we might observe an onion skin under a microscope. The students draw and describe the onion skin cells, and then place a hypertonic salt solution under the coverslip. This can generate numerous questions: "Would the reaction be the same if less salt were added?" "Why didn't every cell react to the solution?" "How big are salt molecules compared to water molecules?" The students are asked, as homework, to select one of the questions, state a hypothesis, and write a procedure for a follow-up lab that might best respond to the question.

Writing Up the Procedures

There are some labs in which the students design a procedure. To prepare them I use exercises such as writing the instructions on how to open their school locker. We can select one set of student instructions and actually try it, following the instructions exactly as written. The students soon learn that writing procedures, like recipe writing, requires a careful attention to all of the details. Describing how to make a peanut butter sandwich is another good exercise.

During a demonstration of an activity, such as showing how to transfer microorganisms from one petri dish to another, I might ask the

FIGURE 6. Writing Up Lab Procedures

<u>Procedure for Placing Water on a Coin</u>

1. First of all, you get a penny, a straw, and some water.

2. Place the penny, head side up, on a flat surface.

3. Suck up some water into the straw and use the straw to drop the water, one drop at a time on the penny.

4. Count how many drops it takes until the water overflows.

5. Repeat at least three times to get an average.

students to write the observed procedure. The results are shared and critiqued.

It is a good idea to have students carefully write up lab safety procedures and place them in their portfolios or notebooks. I know of at least one occasion where following this advice might have saved a teacher from facing a lawsuit.

Another useful exercise makes use of an old lab activity involving trying to determine how many drops of water can be placed on the head of a penny (see Figure 6). The lab groups usually have different results based on variables that include the type of procedure used, the condition of the coin, even the temperature of the room. The list of variables is placed on the board. For homework the students rewrite their procedures, and for each variable they can eliminate they get extra credit.

For most lab activities, the procedure used is the one in the student's lab book. In this case the students do not write the full procedure; instead they write, "Use the procedure on page such-and-such of the lab book," making note of any changes we make.

Learning to Observe

Students are required to write one "backyard" observation each week and place it in their notebooks or portfolios. They may observe anything of their choosing as long as it is biological and within the bounds of good taste (they might observe the activities of birds at a feeder, for example). Initially their descriptions are vague, but as the year progresses both their observation and writing skills improve.

Observation skills can be sharpened in the classroom—for example, each lab team might observe how a crayfish behaves. Two students observe while a third student serves as recorder. They divide their observations into separate lists labeled *fact* and *assumption*. A fact would be "The crayfish moved its chelipeds vigorously"; an assumption would be "The crayfish is agitated." Students learn that facts must be verified, but an assumption can be used without verification as long as it is labeled as such.

Handling Lab Data

Whenever possible, lab data can be expressed in chart or graph form. Many students possess only rudimentary knowledge of how to present information in graph form. The best solution is to inundate them with graphs they can interpret, construct, or base predictions on. Once they have developed graphs using their own data, they can more clearly understand what the authors of other graphs are doing. Students can graph weather information, stock market reports, or sports statistics, among other things. Computer spreadsheet programs can provide students with graphing experience. Have the students write paragraphs interpreting, predicting from, or explaining how to construct graphs.

Writing Conclusions

Most students tend to confuse results with conclusions. I find it useful for the students to think of conclusions as having three parts: the best, most truthful, response to the original question; a reason for the response; and questions that remain. The conclusion in Figure 7 "Observing a Fish," written by a 10th-grade biology student in my class, represents an example of a well-written conclusion.

FIGURE 7. Observing a Fish

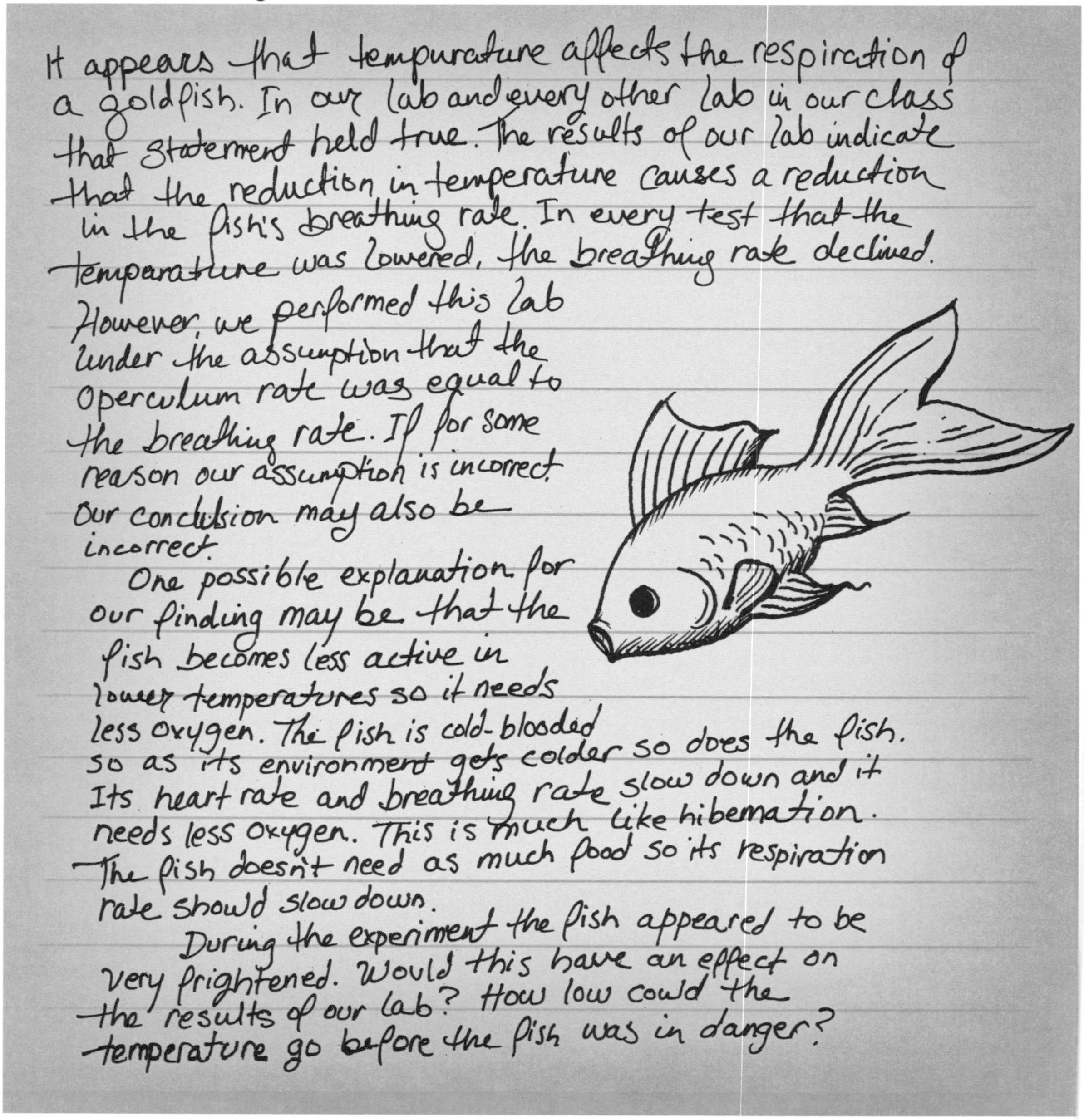

It appears that tempurature affects the respiration of a goldfish. In our lab and every other lab in our class that statement held true. The results of our lab indicate that the reduction in temperature causes a reduction in the fish's breathing rate. In every test that the temperature was lowered, the breathing rate declined. However, we performed this lab under the assumption that the operculum rate was equal to the breathing rate. If for some reason our assumption is incorrect, our conclusion may also be incorrect.

One possible explanation for our finding may be that the fish becomes less active in lower temperatures so it needs less oxygen. The fish is cold-blooded so as its environment gets colder so does the fish. Its heart rate and breathing rate slow down and it needs less oxygen. This is much like hibernation. The fish doesn't need as much food so its respiration rate should slow down.

During the experiment the fish appeared to be very frightened. Would this have an effect on the results of our lab? How low could the temperature go before the fish was in danger?

For further reflection about a lab exercise I sometimes have my students assume the role of a newspaper reporter writing about the lab exercise for the general public. This requires the students to explain *what, where, why, when, who*, and *how*. Writing the piece improves both student writing and thinking.

Open-Ended, Critical-Thinking Exercises

Most people love a mystery and students are no different. Searching scientific journals for solutions that scientists are seeking can produce exercises that not only excite students, but also require them to think through what they already understand. Since there is no "right" answer for the question the students are not intimidated. Their challenge is to find an answer they can defend. The teacher's challenge is to find the research and put it in language the student understands.

My colleague Harry Stookey and I enjoyed getting together to make lessons out of actual scientific data. One lesson requires the students to determine why several thousand trout suddenly died at a lake. The information was taken from a California Department of Fish and Game report. Another lesson involved having the students determine why the king crab population at Kodiak Island, Alaska, was diminishing. Each year we would try to add another research-based lesson to our resource file. Sure, it requires a lot of extra time to develop these lessons, but it's rewarding in several ways: (1) They are lessons that can be used over the years; (2) the students get a better appreciation of how a scientist works; and (3) teaching becomes a creative intellectual endeavor.

For the teacher who does not have the time to create these kinds of lessons, there are federal and state agencies and university sources that might provide help. For example, the National Ocean and Atmospheric Administration (*www.noaa.gov*) and the U.S. Fish & Wildlife Service (*www.fws.gov*. Click on "kids/educators") offer ready-made lessons.

The Tully Monster exercise (Figure 8) is an example of an open-ended science lesson that I have used since 1964 in my biology class to spice up the unit on classification.

Student Research Papers

Students dread writing term papers nearly as much as teachers dread reading them. Students have difficulty defining a topic, and many try to write the report the night before it is due. As a result, they end up handing in their first and only draft. During my early years of teaching, I often read disorganized, poorly written documents that sounded suspiciously similar to an encyclopedia. I marked students' papers as if they were written by professional writers and ended up convincing many students they could not write. I needed to find a better way.

The "I Search" Paper

Deciding the purpose of the term paper is, first, to introduce students to researching for writing and, second, to gain additional knowledge about a subject, I limited their initial draft to a personal account of the research effort. Facts are blended with opinions, theories, and analyses by the student, which results in an honest paper written with the student's voice. The audience is other students. English teachers refer to this assignment as the "I Search" paper.

The "I Search" is the story of the student's progress during the search for topic information. In the paper the student continually asks

FIGURE 8. Tully Monster Exercise

Tully Monster Exercise

Tullimonstrum gregarium ("Tully Monster")
(actual size 91.0 mm)

Background Information

This fossil, *Tullimonstrum gregarium*, was discovered in 1958 in some ironstone slag heaps near a strip mine by Mr. Francis Tully, who took it to the paleontologists at the University of Chicago. The fossils are always found in large numbers, never as a single specimen, and lived in the ocean that covered much of Illinois about 300 million years ago. It is now the official fossil of the state of Illinois. Paleontologists have been trying to unravel some mysteries about this fossil ever since it was discovered.

Read the Following Data Regarding This Fossil and See If You Can Solve Some of the Mystery

1. Other fossils found with *Tullimonstrum gregarium* (popularly known as "Tully Monster") include jellyfish, clams, snails, several types of crustaceans, and even a few insects.
2. Evidence indicates that it was a soft-bodied (except for the transverse bar), segmented animal.

3. Complete specimens have not been found, only fragments.
4. The fossils are fairly common in the Mazon Creek deposits of northeastern Illinois and have recently been found in some of the open-pit mines of the state. *Gregarium* means "common," which explains its species name.
5. Chemical test of the bar organ indicate it is composed of chemicals found in the retina of human eyes.
6. The proboscis contained very small teeth and was not retractable.
7. Tully Monster probably had a complete digestive system and a straight intestine.

The Assignment

Each lab team should submit the best, most appropriate answer they can for each of the following questions. Remember to support your answer with evidence and not confuse fact with assumption.

Questions

1. What phylum should this animal be placed in, or should it have a phylum of its own?
2. Why hasn't Tully Monster been found in other parts of the world?
3. Why is this animal now extinct?
4. What might account for its always being found in groups, never as individuals?
5. How might the age of this fossil be determined?
6. Make a list of questions you have about *Tullimonstrum gregarium*, which, if answered, might help solve some of the mystery of this organism.

Bonus (not required)

If you were going to serve a Tully Monster for dinner, how would you cook it? Write your recipe on a separate piece of paper as it will be submitted to the Home Economics Department for judging. The best recipes will be placed in our classroom's Tully Monster cookbook.

FIGURE 9. Student Map of the Cell

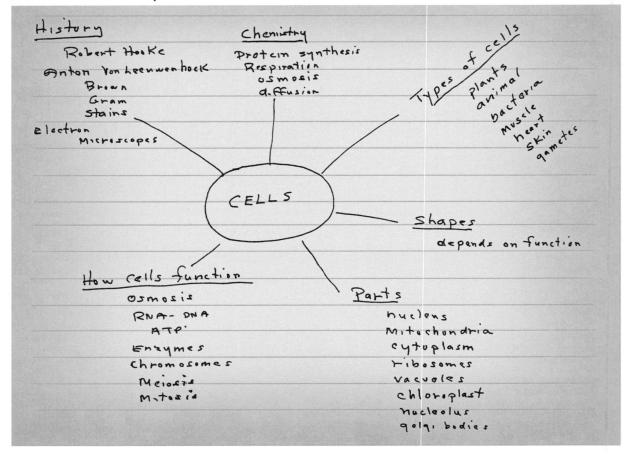

him- or herself the following questions, which form the outline of the paper:

1. What did I want to know?
2. What did I do to obtain the information?
3. What did I learn?
4. What did I think, or feel, about what I learned?
5. What frustrations or difficulties did I have in my search for the information?
6. What questions remain?

If desired, a second draft of the paper can focus on a formal presentation of information with the teacher as audience. The student seeks to explain, in depth, what he or she understands about the topic.

Narrowing the Topic

One of the problems my students have is a failure to narrow their topic. "I want to write about the solar system," a student might say. There are two techniques I have learned that are successful in getting students to narrow their topics and still not discourage them.

Mapping, a technique used by many English teachers, is a good way to narrow the topic of any paper. Students are provided with large pieces of paper and some colored marking pens. In the center of the paper they place the topic they are considering as a subject. Assuming the topic is Cells, a student map might looking something like Figure 9.

From the map, they select an interesting sub-topic and place it at the center of another map. On this map, they number the subtopics in the order in which they will write paragraphs. The students submit the maps to their classmates for comment. Often, students will mention they know someone—a family member, a friend, a public figure—who is knowledgeable about the topic and might assist with the paper.

Another successful method is to have students write down three possible ideas for a paper. Each student goes to the blackboard and writes a single topic that he or she wishes to research. This results in a board full of possible topics. Students might decide to use one of those topics instead of their original choices. Each student heads a piece of paper with the topic he or she has selected and leaves it on his or her desk. The students do a "march around" the room where they look at each other's topics and write down suggestions, questions, and sources of information.

Avoiding Last-Minute Papers

There's nothing like a deadline to stimulate productivity. For a term paper, teachers should ask for three drafts, each with its own deadline. The first draft is submitted about a week after topic selection. The second draft is submitted a month before the paper is due. The total time frame for a typical term paper is three months from assignment to finish.

The first draft can be in any form the student chooses. It does not have to be complete. Some students hand in an outline, others a page or more of rough writing. They must give a sense of what the paper will attempt to convey so that I can ask questions and guide their thinking to some degree.

The second draft is a complete report that needs proofreading. It is reviewed by other students who offer suggestions as to readability and

interest before it is turned in to me for further review.

Only the final draft is graded. Grammar, spelling, and organization are part of the grade. The final document is submitted with the preliminary drafts attached.

Enhancing Science Library Reference Material

Students are encouraged to go beyond the "I Search" paper and submit a manuscript whose goal is to increase understanding and inform a reader outside the classroom about a particular topic. These papers receive extra credit, are placed in a hard cover, and become part of the science room library. For a paper to be accepted, it must be free of misspellings and grammatical errors.

In addition to building up science resources, this is a good way to reward students for their hard work. The students can take great pride in their accomplishments; it's not just another paper that is quickly forgotten, it is a permanent part of the science library collection. It is nice on parent-teacher nights to go to the library and show parents how much their children have achieved. It's even better when former students tell me that doing the extra paper was one of the most beneficial things they did and that the experience helped them a great deal in college.

Managing the Paperwork Load

Cut Down on Correcting

Many teachers, already burdened with excessive paperwork, are reluctant to add more writing exercises to their lessons. I managed to add more writing assignments and also cut my paperwork load by keeping in mind that learning is a process and that too much correcting in the early stages can inhibit student success. If the football coach corrected the quarterback every time he threw a ball in practice, he would convince the quarterback that he couldn't throw.

Every paper needs a response, but the teacher is not always the best responder, especially early on in a new learning unit. Correcting is limited to the papers specifically addressed to me. Students will ask, "Why are we doing these if you don't correct them?" I remind them the football team practices all week, but only the results of the game count; the rest is just for practice. They are aware that missing a practice results in not being allowed to play. They understand they will be doing many assignments for practice, but for me to correct the one that counts they must have all of their practice assignments complete. To manage the task, I make copies of the roll sheets and place them in a binder, called the practice book, where all exercises are recorded. Only those assignments directed to me as audience are graded and go into the official grade book.

The Verbal Response

A verbal response from the teacher is often more effective than a written one. Each student gives me a blank tape cassette at the beginning of the year. I keep them in drawstring bags by period and use them to respond to some some student writing, especially Neuron Notes (see p. 28). Reaching into the bag and grabbing a tape before searching for the student's paper saves time. Students understand the tapes will not be rewound. As I read the student's paper, I talk to him or her on the tape. It is easier than writing long responses and means more to the student. The student gets his or paper back with no marks and listens to the tape—allowing me to

become a personal writing coach! Sometimes, if the focus is on mechanics, the students number each line of their papers so that I can target specific problems in a given paragraph. Since each response takes, on average, two minutes, each tape can hold about 30 responses. Thus each student receives several taped responses during the school year.

An additional advantage of using the tapes is that a parent can listen to the tape with his or her child, allowing them to share the lesson. Both parent and child learn together, and my relationship with both is enhanced.

A few former students have told me that they kept their tapes and listened to them while they studied biology in college. "We can listen to you explain fundamental principles of biology all over again. We can hear your dog barking and your wife telling you to take out the garbage, and we can listen to all those terrible jokes again," they tell me.

Golden Lines

Each student, armed with a marking pen, selects the Golden Line (see p. 7) on another student's paper and highlights it. He or she reads the line aloud to the author and explains why the line was chosen. The writer has the satisfaction of a positive response, and the teacher does not have to lug the papers home and "correct" them.

Typical of a golden line is a selection from one of my Basic Science students, who wrote, "A volcano is a zit on the face of the earth." Golden lines can generate active, student-owned discussions. All golden lines are placed on a section of the bulletin board labeled "The Wall of Fame," as represented in Figure 10.

Single-Purpose Papers

Corrections should focus entirely on the stated purpose of the paper; marking a paper for mul-

FIGURE 10. A "Wall of Fame"

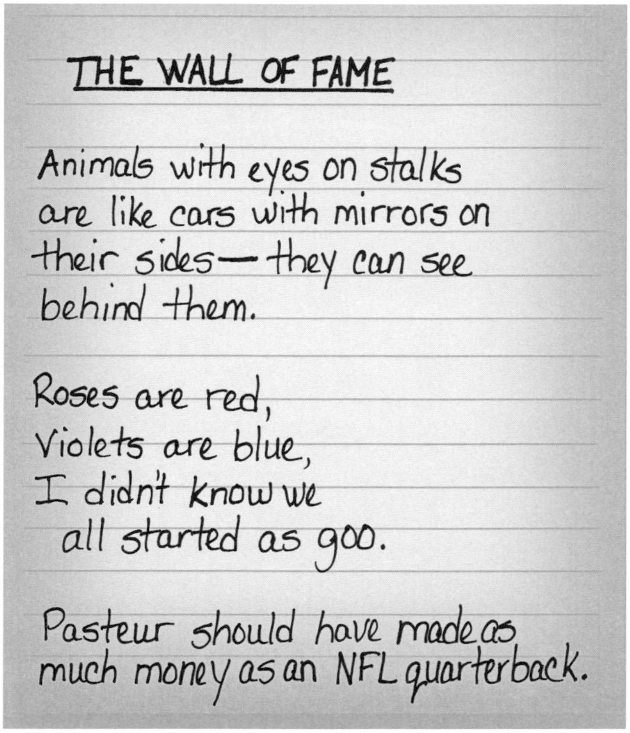

> THE WALL OF FAME
>
> Animals with eyes on stalks are like cars with mirrors on their sides — they can see behind them.
>
> Roses are red,
> Violets are blue,
> I didn't know we
> all started as goo.
>
> Pasteur should have made as much money as an NFL quarterback.

tiple purposes tends to confuse the students. I have several stamps, each designating the specific purpose of an assignment. One stamp says, "Checked for organization only"; another tells the student the paper has been checked only for content, and another says, "Uncorrected first draft." There's even one stamp that tells the student the paper was only checked for mechanical errors such as spelling and grammar.

The Log Keeper

One problem I faced was dealing with students who missed class. They had a tendency to crowd around my desk while I was trying to get attendance forms filled out and simultaneously get the class going. They asked questions like, "I was absent for three days. Did you do anything important while I was gone?" I had to explain what they missed and provide them with a makeup assignment. More often than not, I told

them, "Write a report" or "Answer the questions in the back of the chapter." These assignments increased my paperwork load and taught the students very little.

I solved this problem by asking for volunteers to keep a one-page log of each day's activities, using extra credit as an enticement. Each day, a different student writes the log as homework. The log is written for a particular audience: the students who were not in class the day of the log. The log must be clearly written so the absent student does not have any questions (Figure 11).

The log is placed on the bulletin board and a copy is given to the teacher. Each log keeper, in turn, removes the old log and places it in a binder. There is a binder for each class. A student who may have missed several days checks the binder. The resulting notebook becomes a student-written record of what transpired each day. It is particularly useful in showing administrators or parents what the students have been doing.

The log is also an excellent source of questions and information for later classroom research by the teacher. Teachers need to ask themselves to what extent a lesson succeeded, or failed, and attempt to determine the reasons why. The teacher gathers evidence, which can include observations, interviews, student work, test results, class logs, student portfolios, and journal notes. Ideally the teacher should share, through publication, the results of his or her findings. *The Science Teacher*, a magazine for high school science teachers published by the National Science Teachers Association, is an example of a periodical that seeks articles from classroom researchers.

This Year's Papers: Samples for Next Year

I collect papers for use as models for *future* classes. When I go through the stack, I place an

FIGURE 11. A Student Log Entry

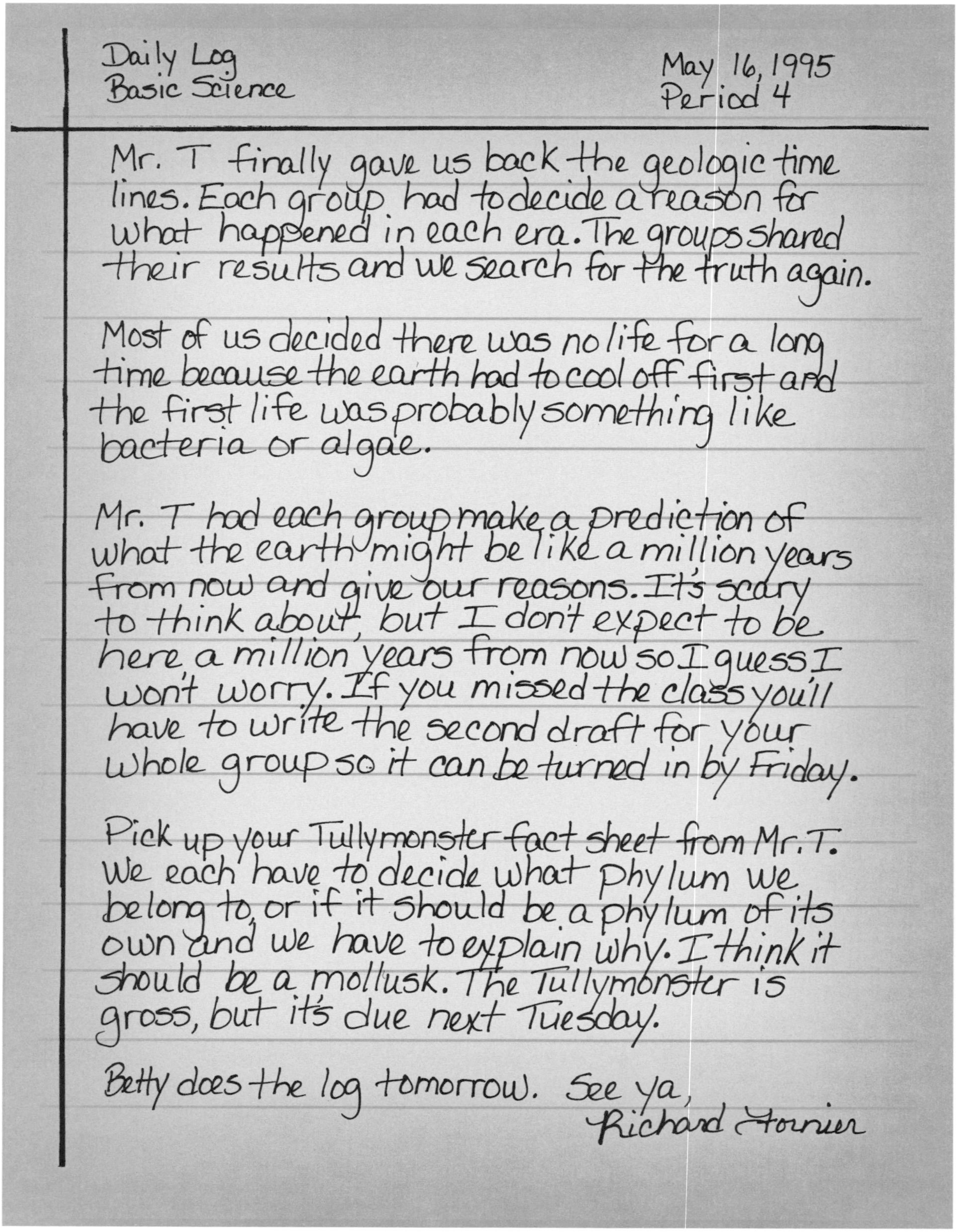

Daily Log   May 16, 1995
Basic Science   Period 4

Mr. T finally gave us back the geologic time lines. Each group had to decide a reason for what happened in each era. The groups shared their results and we search for the truth again.

Most of us decided there was no life for a long time because the earth had to cool off first and the first life was probably something like bacteria or algae.

Mr. T had each group make a prediction of what the earth might be like a million years from now and give our reasons. It's scary to think about, but I don't expect to be here a million years from now so I guess I won't worry. If you missed the class you'll have to write the second draft for your whole group so it can be turned in by Friday.

Pick up your Tullymonster fact sheet from Mr. T. We each have to decide what phylum we belong to, or if it should be a phylum of its own and we have to explain why. I think it should be a mollusk. The Tullymonster is gross, but it's due next Tuesday.

Betty does the log tomorrow.   See ya,
                                    Richard Fournier

asterisk (*) on every fifth paper, indicating to the student I would like to have the paper returned. Some students return them, some don't. The quality of the paper doesn't matter—they can be good, bad, or mediocre. I make overhead transparencies of the papers that can be used in later years in a variety of ways. Since the papers do not represent the work of students who are present, students feel free to critique the papers without fear of embarrassment. The students give each paper a letter grade and write a paragraph justifying the grade. This is followed by a discussion and group consensus. I return their own ungraded papers and direct them to give their papers a grade based on the criteria we have set forth as a class. They write a one-paragraph defense of their grade.

Often, when an assignment is given, I show some overheads of good papers from past years to indicate how a paper should look. This is especially helpful to the visual learners. I can also use the papers to teach students about the mistakes they are making. A useful exercise is to circle a sentence on an old paper and ask the students to tell me what is wrong with it. This results in a mini-lesson in grammar, punctuation, spelling, or sentence structure.

Student activities that are not immediately evaluated by the teacher may be placed in the students' notebooks or portfolios, where the student can evaluate his or her own work before submitting a progress report to the teacher for a grade.

Alleviating Parental Concerns

A paradoxical thing occurred as I shifted from putting a lot of marks on papers to my new methods of evaluation. The students enjoyed my classes and learned more. I found teaching to be more rewarding. However, parents weren't always pleased. This was not like the school they remembered. Some probably thought I had retired without informing the school board.

To alleviate their concerns, I invited parents to an hour-long workshop called "Why I am not going to correct all of those papers anymore." The parent workshop is best held a few days after the school holds its annual open house. Over coffee and doughnuts, I explain my teaching and student assessment methods, asking parents to write, share, and discuss the merits of my strategy. Those who are not convinced are at least assured that I am not just avoiding work.

Wrapping Up a Unit

It's time to conclude our unit and determine what the students have learned. In too many science classrooms, testing is the only way learning is measured. Successful teachers know learning is deeper than most tests can measure, so they ascertain the depth of understanding through a variety of methods: tests, lab observations, noting the type of questions students ask, and writing and reading assignments. Many science teachers rely on student portfolios for a better understanding of student success. See John Dorroh's discussion (on pp. 31–34) of the use of portfolios in the science classroom.

When tests are used I find the short essay, combined with a few well-developed multiple-choice questions, to be effective.

Reviews

When I mention review in class, students' shoulders slump and they mumble, "He's going to tell us again." The way to overcome this skepticism is to place the review process in the students' hands. At least a week prior to the exam, I march into class carrying large sheets of paper and coffee cans full of marking pens. The students, working in groups of three, produce large colorful drawings depicting their understanding of the subject. One group, deciding to represent cell energy in terms of rock and roll, drew a picture of an electric guitar and an amplifier (Figure 12). The guitar, representing the energy source, was labeled *photosynthesis*. The guitar strings were called *light, water, carbon dioxide*, and *chlorophyl*. The amplifier, labled *respiration*, represented how a cell utilized the energy.

Each group shows and explains their drawings to the class, providing an excellent student-owned review. I have an easy day because the students are doing the teaching; more importantly, I can determine if I have adequately prepared the students for a test. The drawings remain on display for several days.

Neuron Notes

The homework that follows the presentation of the drawings requires each student to write a one-page summary of what he or she understands about the subject. Students are instructed not to refer to the text or their notes. This assignment is

FIGURE 12. A Student Drawing: Cell Energy and Rock and Roll

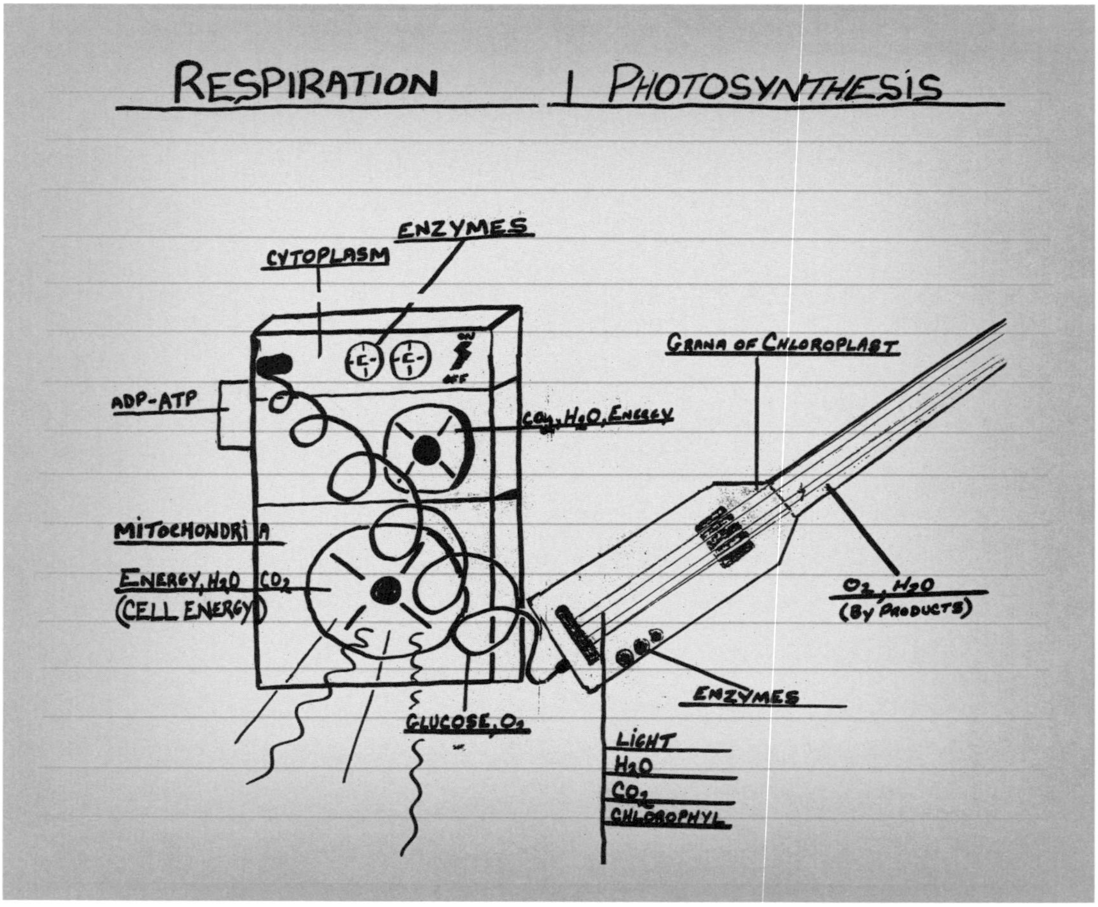

called a Neuron Note because it requires thinking. At first students are reluctant to admit what they do not understand; however, this reluctance fades when they realize the purpose of the Neuron Notes is to discover what they don't understand. Revealing what they don't understand exposes what they need to study the most. The Neuron Note is like a pre-write exercise for a test.

Essay Tests

Essay tests work best when the question is carefully thought out. When I first began teaching, I posed questions such as, "Explain what you know about cells." Many students froze up, writing little or wandering off topic. Others simply wrote down everything that came to mind without regard to organization. As a result, this type of question often produced papers that were nearly impossible to score.

A better essay question is: "Contrast a plant cell with an animal cell, and give reasons why they differ. Be sure to use specific examples to support your statements." I keep test essay responses short, usually a half page, with each question worth 10 points.

It is vital for the teacher to take the essay test *with* the students for three reasons: First, it affirms, for the teacher, the focus of the question; second, it indicates the fairness of the question; and third, it provides a rubric to be used when the test is returned.

Holistic Scoring

The test is scored using a variation of the holistic process. In true holistic scoring, a team of examiners reads each paper rapidly. Each examiner places a score in one corner of the paper, folding the corner over so the next examiner cannot see the mark. The different scores are averaged out to provide a single grade.

In my variation of holistic scoring, I have only one reader (me), but I read the tests with the same rapidity as the holistic examiner and can quickly score an entire class set.

The value of holistic scoring is that it allows me to obtain an initial impression of each test that focuses on what you might call "The Big Picture." I get an overall sense of what each student is trying to say and how well he or she said it, without having to concentrate on narrow issues such as grammar, punctuation, and spelling. The students benefit by getting a rapid feedback on their work that concentrates on the substance of what they are saying.

Challenge Day

I hold a "challenge day" when the test is returned. I read my own test effort to the class. This becomes the rubric for the students as they compare their own efforts to mine. If a student feels cheated, he or she raises as hand and declares a challenge. The student then reads his or her answer out and I reconsider my score.

A challenge is always risky because the student might gain *or lose* points. I make my judgment based on what the student wrote, not on any later explanations of what they "really meant." This often results in a class discussion with students sometimes acting as jury.

Challenge day provides a first-rate review of the entire unit. The test is no longer simply a test; it's an opportunity to show off. As the semester moves on, the students' writing and thinking becomes sharper.

Concluding Remarks

Despite what teacher evaluation forms suggest, there is no single formula for successful teaching. Keith Caldwell, the single best classroom teacher I have ever observed, says:

The bottom line in teaching is, and will always

remain, the art and the genius of that particular teacher, in that particular classroom, with that particular group of students, on that particular day.

If we can be assured a professional teacher steps into each classroom, the dedicated professional will continually experiment, learn, and grow as he or she finds a way that is effective.

Selected Bibliography

Berthoff, A. E., ed. 1983. *Reclaiming the imagination: Philosophical perspectives for writers and teachers of writing.* See J. R. Oppenheimer, "Analogy of science," pp. 189–202, and N. W. Pirie, "Selecting facts and avoiding assumptions," pp. 203–211. Portsmouth, NH: Boynton/Cook.

These two articles provided a philosophical basis for the author's views and pedagogical approach to writing in the science classroom.

Francis, L. 2000. *Sustainable Seas Expeditions, Teacher Resource Book.* Available online at *www.nationalgeographic.com/seas.* Hard copies are available through the National Oceanic and Atmospheric Administration's National Marine Sanctuary Program; send an e-mail to sally.ziegler@noaa.gov for more information.

This book is a collection of teacher-tested lessons designed for student exploration of scientific problems involved with oceanography and marine biology. The science teacher will find it a valuable list of resources.

MacLean, M., and M. Mohr. 1999. *Teacher researchers at work.* Berkeley, CA: National Writing Project.

This is an excellent resource and guide for any teacher who wants to do some classroom research. The authors explore, and show examples of, research efforts by a variety of teachers.

Olson, C. B. 2002. *The reading/writing connection: Strategies for teaching and learning in the secondary classroom.* Boston, MA: Allyn and Bacon.

This book is probably the best methods resource available for any teacher who wishes to emphasize reading and writing. The science teacher will find the following chapters very useful: Chapter 5, "Strategies for interacting with a text"; Chapter 8, "Writing across the curriculum"; and Chapter 12, "Assessing students' progress."

Pizzini, E. L., S. K. Abell, and D. S. Shepardson. 1988. Rethinking thinking in the science classroom: A thoughtful curriculum. *The Science Teacher* (Dec.): 22–25.

This interesting article insists that processing skills are more important than rote memorization in the successful science classroom

Rico, G. L. 1997. Clustering: A prewriting process. In *Practical ideas for teaching writing at the high school and college level,* ed. C. B. Olson. Sacramento, CA: California Department of Education.

Gabriel Rico, the guru of the clustering and mapping technique, shares practical approaches for using that technique that are applicable across the curriculum.

Wotring, A., and R. Tierney. 1981. *Two studies of writing in high school science.* Classroom Research Study #5. Berkeley, CA: Bay Area Writing Project, University of California-Berkeley.

English teacher Ann Wotring enrolled in a high school chemistry class, a course she had never taken before. She applied "writing to think" techniques to assist her own learning and worked with other students on the use of the techniques. She reports on her success and failures with it. Science teacher Robert Tierney describes a more traditional, empirical study to determine if writing activities helped students to better understand, and retain, science concepts. The conclusions reached in both these studies have implications for science teachers.

Zinsser, W. 1988. *Writing to learn.* New York: Harper and Row.

This is one of the best written books about the subject in print. Zinsser, believing that writing, thinking, and learning are the same process, describes his own early struggle with learning scientific and technical concepts. As a writer, however, he realized that writing articles about technology allowed him to overcome his fears and learn the subject matter. His discussions with professors of physics, chemistry, biology, and mathematics should be of particular interest to science teachers. If you can read only one book about writing across the curriculum, this is the book.

How Science Portfolio Assessment Can Improve Student Writing

By John Dorroh

National standards in science require that teachers use instructional methods other than lecturing and that students be assessed using methods other than paper-and-pencil tests, which tend to limit what is being measured. This is not to say that lecturing and written testing are inherently bad; they are not. But deliberate orchestration must be used to ensure that these are not the sole teaching-learning methods in the classroom.

Different assessment techniques need to be used over time to give a more accurate and truthful picture of what students know about science. Portfolio assessment is one such technique.

Background

I had noticed for many years as a biology teacher that my students did not identify with being a scientist. As a matter of fact, they seemed downright belligerent when I insisted that all of them were indeed budding scientists. Statements such as "I'm no scientist! They're all a bunch of nerds!" typically surfaced. When they wrote compositions during the first week of school entitled, "How I See Myself as a Scientist," there was widespread defiance with the message that scientists are forgetful, strange, odd in appearance, and stuck in a lab with smoking test tubes and bottles of foul-smelling mixtures. *Had Hollywood and TV done this to our children?* I asked myself.

Then, in the early 1990s I embarked upon a program of portfolio assessment with the purpose of changing my students' negative images of scientists and the work that they do into something more positive.

My normal workload was already unbelievably heavy. With about 140–150 students, grades 9–10 (Biology II and Anatomy & Physiology), I simply could not add another major program into my curriculum, no matter how good it might be

for the students. My interest was piqued, however, by hearing about various portfolio programs—both successful and unsuccessful—around the country. So, with a determination to streamline my workload, I embarked upon a new journey that made *me* feel like a real scientist.

My support group was the 35 teacher/consultants at the Mississippi Writing/Thinking Institute, located on the campus of Mississippi State University (MSU) in northeast Mississippi, one of the 185 sites for the National Writing Project. Mary Ann Smith, the director of the California Writing Project, and Sandra Burkett from MSU served as facilitators. Mary Ann had become somewhat of an expert on the subject of writing for portfolios, had written a book with Nancy Murphy (*Writing Portfolios: A Bridge from Teaching to Assessment,* The Pippin Teacher's Library, 1991), and came to Mississippi in 1991 to start another statewide "pioneer" group. We met as a mixed-level-all-disciplines group for four days and then received the charge to start a portfolio program in our individual classrooms. We would have two follow-up meetings during the school year and have an end-of-the year session on the Mississippi Gulf Coast. Since portfolio assessment was brand-new to 90% of us, we had no road maps to follow. We would be offering each other suggestions and feedback along the way.

A term I heard repeatedly from the individuals in this pioneer portfolio team was *portfolio culture.* "What is that?" I asked. Because portfolio assessment was so new to this group of 35 educators, only a few had a real idea of how to respond. One teacher who had had some experience told us that once we got our programs started, the classroom would have a new atmosphere, especially on days when we were working on specific portfolio assignments. I did not quite understand what she was talking about, but I was willing to try it out as

I began to collect my data and anecdotes. After all, this was my own personal science experiment. It was exciting and a bit scary since I did not know exactly where this road would lead.

Helping Students Become Reflective Learners

Today, having used portfolios in my science classes for over 12 years, I feel that I could not exist as a teacher without them. They do indeed help my students to see themselves as scientists, which was my original purpose. Portfolios

- help students to connect to their work throughout the year, giving them a well-defined focus;
- are powerful assessment tools, which are tied in closely to the teacher's purpose for using them;
- can change the atmosphere in the classroom, resulting in identifiable behaviors, collectively called "portfolio culture";
- promote critical thinking among students;
- open doors by providing opportunities such as working with a partner for a common goal, letting students express themselves artistically, and giving them autonomy in the decision-making process;
- can serve as a vehicle for documentation of science concepts taught and mastered by the student and to what degree;
- help students to become reflective learners; and
- give the teacher a broader perspective of a student's strengths and abilities in science than traditional assessment tools.

Portfolios in Action

Here is how it works. Every student has his or her own manila folder in a box set aside for each of my six classes. We appropriately call these "collecting folders." The students' names are on the tabs, and the folders are arranged alphabetically. Each time that I return a paper to the students, they are responsible for filing it in their folder. I do not allow them to file items while I am giving instructions or providing content (e.g., lecturing, conducting a game/review, facilitating a discus-

sion). Instead they are free to file papers during small-group work sessions, before the bell rings for class to begin, or after a laboratory session. I also urge them to make sure that they file every item that I return since part of their overall grade comes from the contents of the folders. The more items that are in the collecting files, the better.

Approximately once a month I instruct my students to take their collecting folders and select one item that best shows them thinking, writing, or behaving like a scientist. Some months I am more specific and tell them to find their best graph, or their best lab activity, for instance.

Next, I instruct them to share the contents of their folders with a partner and to help each other to select their item of the month. After the sharing and selecting, each student becomes a reflective learner by responding to the questions on a self-evaluation sheet (see "Self-Evaluation for Portfolio Selections," p. 33).

Once this is done, they staple the three components (the cover sheet, the piece that was evaluated, and the self-evaluation sheet) together in the upper-left-hand corner and place them into their portfolio folders. Every student also has his or her own portfolio folder, which is housed in a separate box from their collecting files. Every box is clearly labeled to prevent confusion and misplacement of the different folders. (This portfolio folder is different from the collecting folder and students have a bit of trouble at first remembering this.)

I have noticed that on days when the students are making selections, the overall tone of the class changes. This is part of what that teacher/consultant in the Writing Project had called "portfolio culture." For one thing, the vast majority of the students have no trouble staying focused on the assignment. They seem to enjoy looking through their work and sharing it with a partner. Most of them keep the same partner throughout the year, giving them some continuity. Others may have to change, with my assistance, due to personality clashes. Occasionally a student prefers to work alone, and that is not a problem.

The demeanor of the class changes when students are engaged in a selection session. I hear them being more honest and "up-front," with questions such as "Tommy, why are you selecting *that* item? This one [pointing] is so much better. It really does show you using all of your science skills, man." I hear them being more reflective: "Tanya, I think you deserved a better grade on that project. Look at how detailed your observations were!" And "I wish I could go back and retake that test. I would have put more effort into it." There is a productive buzz in the room as they support one another throughout the session.

Later in the year I take pictures of the students in the lab or while they are engaged in some other activity. These are positioned and glued or taped onto the front of their portfolio folders, personalizing them in an appealing manner. Some add color with pens and markers and then draw a bubble to show what they are thinking about being a scientist. As the year progresses the portfolios begin to take on lives of their own. They really do begin to let the students see themselves as budding scientists, as I always encourage them to do.

The Teacher and Portfolio Evaluation

Just as there is not one way to implement a portfolio program for your science classroom, there is certainly not one way to evaluate the portfolios. How you decide to evaluate them should be a reflection of your style of teaching and assessing and should also feel comfortable for your students. You can "grade-as-you-go," assigning a number of points (such as 10 points) to each monthly entry

that the student has selected and evaluated and reflected upon. Or you can wait to assign one overall grade at the end of the school year. You can use a rubric that you and your students have designed or select one from an online source or a teacher resource book.

I assign credit checks to each completed monthly selection as we move through the school year, and then give a major grade for the whole project in May, just before school is over for the year. A credit check is simply a special mark placed directly on each monthly entry that tells the student that it has been "credited to his/her account." In my grade book there are many credit checks for various assignments and projects, not just for portfolio entries. Each grading period I decide how many credit checks it will take for a student to receive a "big grade," sort of like an upgrade on an airline flight.

I use this system of credit checks because my students demand a grade or some kind of mark on almost everything we do. I understand their rationale: They've worked hard and they want some acknowledgment of that. However, it is virtually impossible to give a number grade on every item for every student. Plus, it is not always in their best interest to assign a grade in the middle of an ongoing assignment. My friend Bob Tierney, a former science teacher and coach from Fremont, California (and main author of the book you are reading), used to explain to his students, and now

---

Self-Evaluation for Portfolio Selections
Month:_____   School Year:_____
Please respond to the following items in complete sentences and with a significant degree of detail.
1. What is the name of this month's selection, or what is an appropriate description of it?
2. Why did you choose this particular selection?
3. What did you like about it (enough to have selected it)?
4. What could you have done to make the selection even better?
5. If you had to take the selection one step further, what would you do?
6. How does this selection allow you to see yourself as a scientist?
7. How does this selection allow you to see yourself as a better thinker?
8. How does this selection allow you to see yourself as a better writer?

I do the same, that you do not get a "grade" for coming to practice for football every day. Yes, you do have to be there, and you do get "credit" for being there. But the big "grade" is assigned on Friday night when the ball game is played in front of an audience. My students seem to accept and like that explanation.

What I do is give them a credit check for each item completed at the time the grading period is coming to a close. Once an item is placed in the portfolio folder, it is finished. However, it is not uncommon for students to take portfolio items out of the portfolio folder and work on them independently to make them even better. Remember that only finished pieces (ones that have been selected through discussion with a partner and that have undergone self-evaluation) go in the portfolio folders.

In May, when the portfolio is completed, I expect there to be 10 items inside the portfolio folder. I count each item as 10 points, for a total of 100 points. I use that grade as a major project grade. In the case of a student who is borderline failing/passing, I can justify his or her passing based on the work in the portfolio. You have to decide how you will assess your students' portfolios. If your school has strict guidelines for assigning grades, meet with your administrators and discuss your guidelines, which should be in writing and distributed to parents and students at the beginning of the school year.

Reflections

Since my involvement with the National Writing Project, I have learned to become more of a risk-taker and a facilitator. My writing-based classroom has become a living laboratory, so to speak, where communities of learners begin to plan and do science. They write, collect, select, and reflect with regularity. Over the last decade I have seen reluctant writers become more fluent with their journal entries. I have witnessed the "wait time" between the announcement of the writing prompt and the time my students began writing decrease, and I have heard them say that writing in their other classes became easier since they had practiced in their science class.

Incorporating portfolios helps to soften the resistance that students often have for science. It's like holding up a mirror and taking a look at what they see. Sometimes they like the reflection and are encouraged to continue their good work; sometimes they do not like what they see and decide to change.

Another bonus that comes from using portfolios is that I always find out something new about my students. It might be about a hobby that incorporates science principles or the fact that a particular student loves going to natural science museums. Once I learned that a student's aunt was a botanist who specialized in local flora, so we invited her in for a series of sessions. I always can detect who has problems with language and can work with the language arts teacher to help the student correct his or her problems.

Finally, portfolios can help pull a lot of loose pieces together. Not only is my original goal met—showing students how they themselves can behave like scientists—but I have seen a marked improvement in their overall writing on science topics. I believe that once habits of mind have been established, such as reflecting on one's work, students begin to naturally go deeper into their content, which shows up in their writing, including essays and reports.

Has it all been a bed of roses? No, not at all. Change usually brings a degree of frustration, some resistance, and even a bit of resentment. But using portfolios in science to help evaluate my writing-based science classes has given my last decade of teaching more meaning for me...and for the budding scientists with whom I have had the pleasure to work.

> **Web sites about the Use of Portfolios**
> *www.accessexcellence.org/21st/TL/mahood_port.html*
> *www.ash.udel.edu/ash/teacher/portfolio.html*
> *www.geocities.com/Athens/Delphi/1993/rubrics/teresa/rubrics.htm#6*

Acknowledgments

I wish to thank James Gray, former director of the National Writing Project (now retired) for letting an old biology teacher join the ranks; Mary K. Healy, co-director, Puente Project, University of California at Berkeley, for encouraging me to explore writing-to-learn; Pat D'Arcy, British Writing Project, for inspiring me with her wisdom and energy; Mary Ann Smith, co-director, National Writing Project, for sharing her interest and concern; Francis P. Collea, director of Research and Sponsored Programs, California State University, Long Beach, for encouraging me to initiate this project and providing advice as it progressed; and Keith Caldwell, veteran teacher of English (now retired), Fremont Unified Schools, Fremont, California, my mentor.

The following individuals provided specific ideas and techniques that I found very useful:
- Laury Fischer, instructor, Diablo Valley College: The "walk around" to initiate a paper.
- Dr. Dixie Goswami, Auburn University: Activity to explore student apprehensions.
- Rebecca Kaplan, coordinator, language arts, Oakland Public Schools: The pre-write activity for argumentative essay.
- Dorothy Letcher, English teacher, Fremont Unified Schools: Use of cassette tapes for responding to student writing.
- Lee Swenson, social studies teacher, Aragon High School, San Mateo, CA: Simile drawings for review.
- Liz Simon, University of California: Students writing about their names.

———Bob Tierney

About the Authors

Bob Tierney has been called "one of the gurus of writing across the curriculum." He taught high school science in Fremont, California, for 32 years and has served as a teacher and consultant for the National Writing Project since 1980.

John Dorroh has taught science at high schools in Georgia and Mississippi, where he pioneered portfolio assessment. He is also a teacher and consultant with the Mississippi Writing/Thinking Institute at Mississippi State University, one of the model sites for the National Writing Project.